A Proverbial Alphabet

Words of Wisdom for the Ages from the Book of Proverbs

Compiled by Janet Gauthier
Photography by
Janet Gauthier and Annette Simon

Christianity Every Day
Albuquerque, New Mexico

A Proverbial Alphabet: Words of Wisdom for the Ages from the Book of Proverbs

Janet Gauthier and Annette Simon

ISBN: 978-0-578-40405-9

Copyright © 2018 by Janet Gauthier

Published by Christianity Every Day, United States of America
www.christianityeveryday.com

All rights reserved. No part of this publication may be reproduced, stored in a retrieval system, or transmitted in any form or by any means: electronic, mechanical, photocopy, recording, or otherwise without prior permission of the author, unless permitted under Sections 107 or 108 of the 1976 United States Copyright Act.

"Scripture quotations marked (ESV) are from The ESV® Bible (The Holy Bible, English Standard Version®), copyright © 2001 by Crossway, a publishing ministry of Good News Publishers. Used by permission. All rights reserved."

Scripture quotations marked (NIV) are taken from the Holy Bible, New International Version®, NIV®. Copyright © 1973, 1978, 1984, 2011 by Biblica, Inc.™ Used by permission of Zondervan. All rights reserved worldwide. www.zondervan.com The "NIV" and "New International Version" are trademarks registered in the United States Patent and Trademark Office by Biblica, Inc.™

"Scripture quotations marked (The Message) are taken from The Message. Copyright Â© 1993, 1994, 1995, 1996, 2000, 2001, 2002. Used by permission of NavPress Publishing Group."

Introduction

I have always loved reading because it takes me to places that I may never get to see in person. Reading lets me dream. So much so that I came to believe that perhaps I could write a book. So, several years ago this vision began to take shape and the idea for a children's' book came to life. Thus, "A Proverbial Alphabet" was born. It soon became more than a children's' book, it became a book of insights and wisdom for anyone of any age. And the best part? It was already written -- by the greatest Author! The hardest part? Choosing just *one* verse from the book of Proverbs for each letter in the alphabet. And, because I am a visual learner I wanted to provide a "picture" of what that verse might "look" like. I hope you enjoy reading this book as much as I've enjoyed putting it all together. I also hope that you might use it to inspire thoughtful conversations and discussions with your family or friends or help you find solutions for everyday problems in life.

I am so thankful to my wonderful friend Annette who contributed several of her inspiring and creative photographs that helped bring the book to fruition. I am very thankful for my two sisters and four brothers who have always been there to lend support and encouragement during the highs and lows of life.

And most of all I want to thank God for my three children who provided me with countless photographic opportunities and reminders of God's love, care and provision.

Janet Gauthier

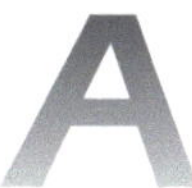

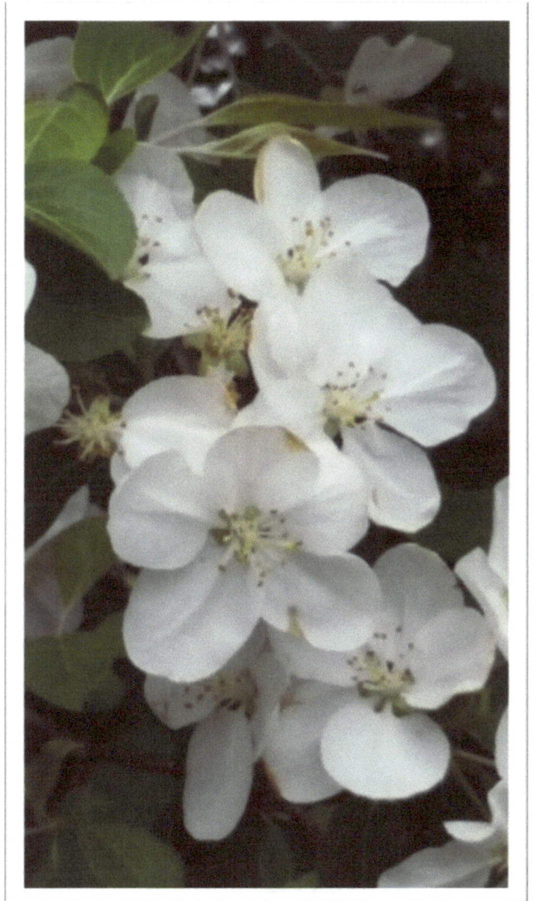

Apple Blossoms Photo: Janet Gauthier

A **gentle *answer* turns away wrath, but a harsh word stirs up *anger*.**

Proverbs 15:1 (NIV)

B

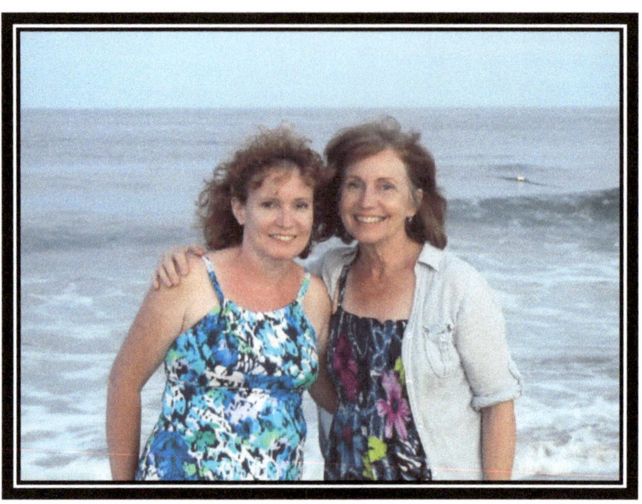

Photo: Janet Gauthier

Charm is deceitful, and *beauty* is vain, but a woman who fears the LORD is to be praised
Proverbs 31:30 (ESV)

C

Even small *children* are known by their actions, so is their *conduct* really pure and upright?
Proverbs 20:11 (NIV)

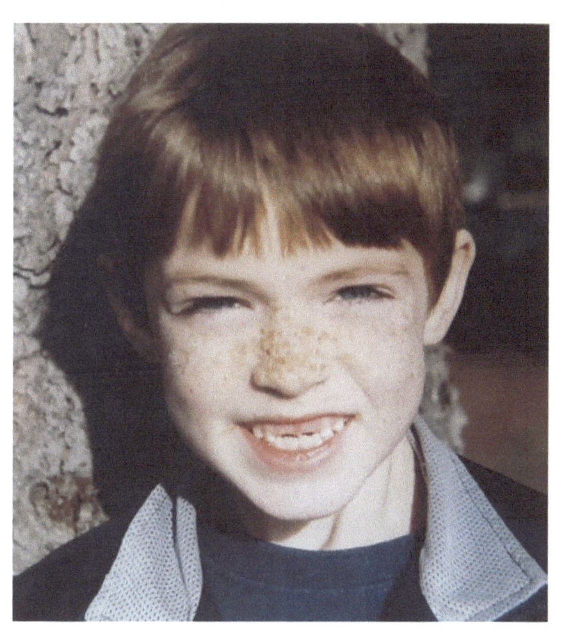

Photo: Janet Gauthier

D

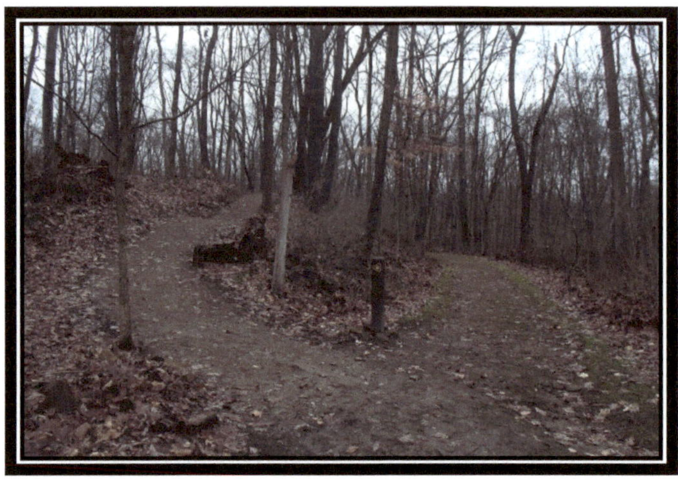

Photo: Annette Simon

Without good *direction*, people lose their way; the more wise counsel you follow, the better your chances.
Proverbs 11:14 (The Message)

E

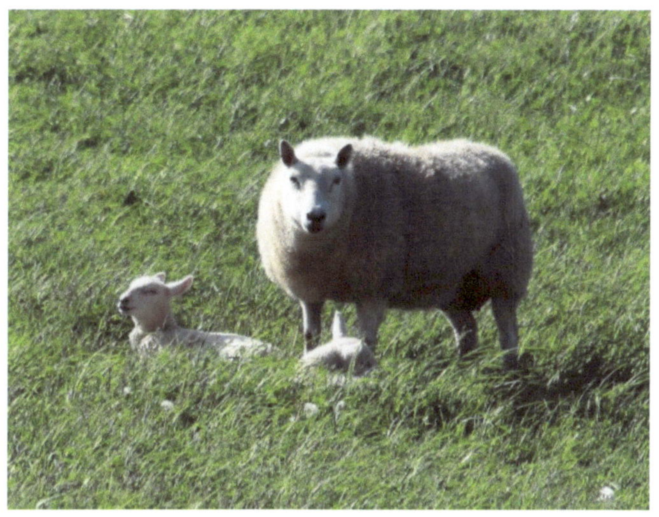

Photo: Annette Simon

Ears **that hear and** ***eyes*** **that see –**
The LORD has made them both.
Proverbs 20:12 (NIV)

F

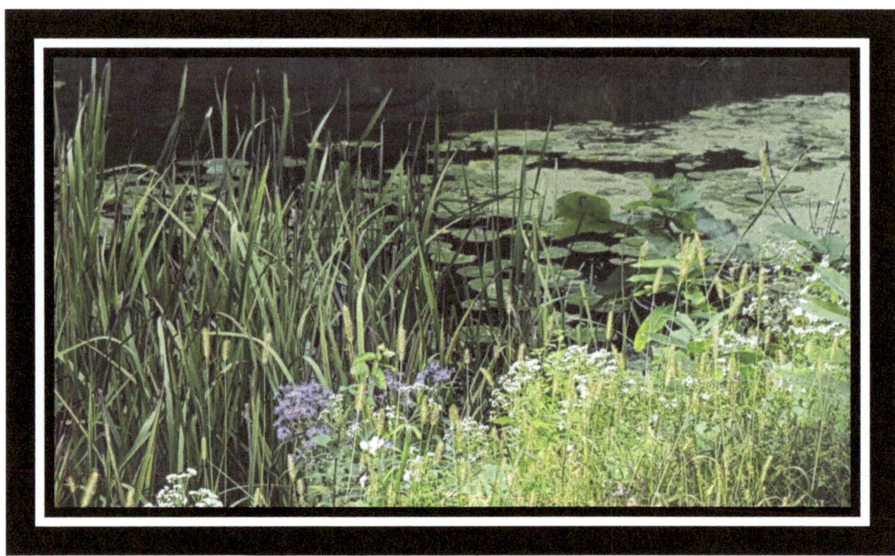

Photo: Janet Gauthier

You can't *find firm footing* in a swamp, but life rooted in God stands *firm*.

Proverbs 12:3 (The Message)

G

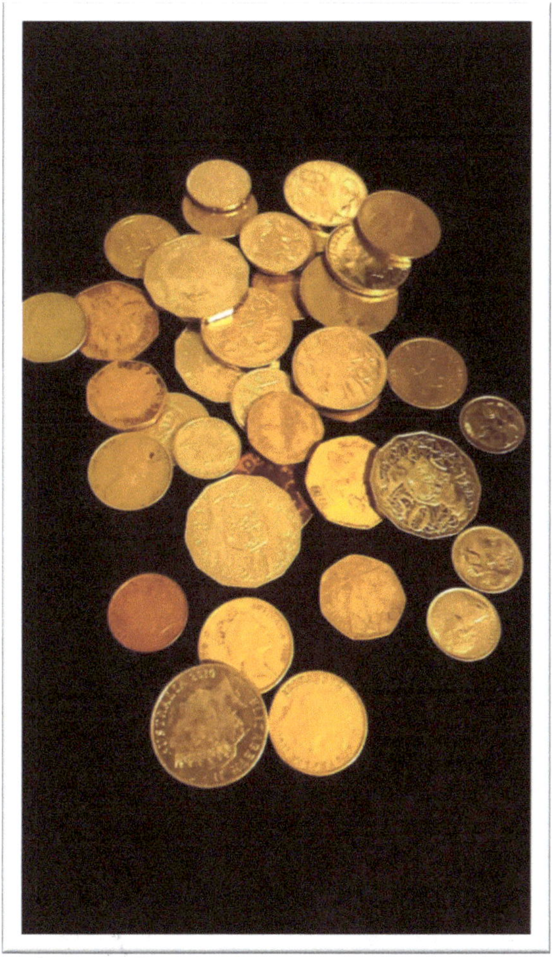

Photo: Janet Gauthier

A *good* name is
more
desirable than
great riches;
to be
esteemed is
better than
silver or *gold*.
Proverbs 22:1 (NIV)

H

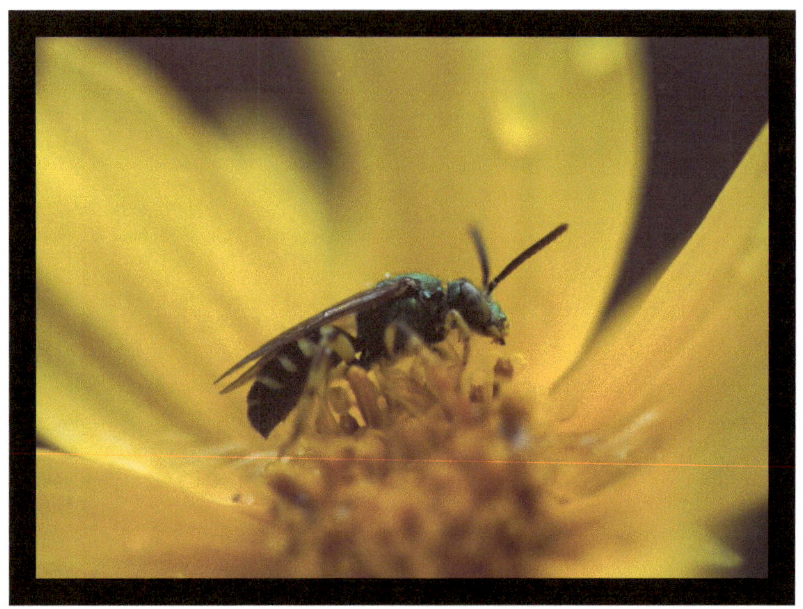

Photo: Annette Simon

Gracious words are a *honeycomb*,
sweet to the soul and
***healing* to the bones.**
Proverbs 16:24 (NIV)

I

Whoever walks in *integrity* walks securely, but whoever takes crooked paths will be found out.

Proverbs 10:9 (NIV)

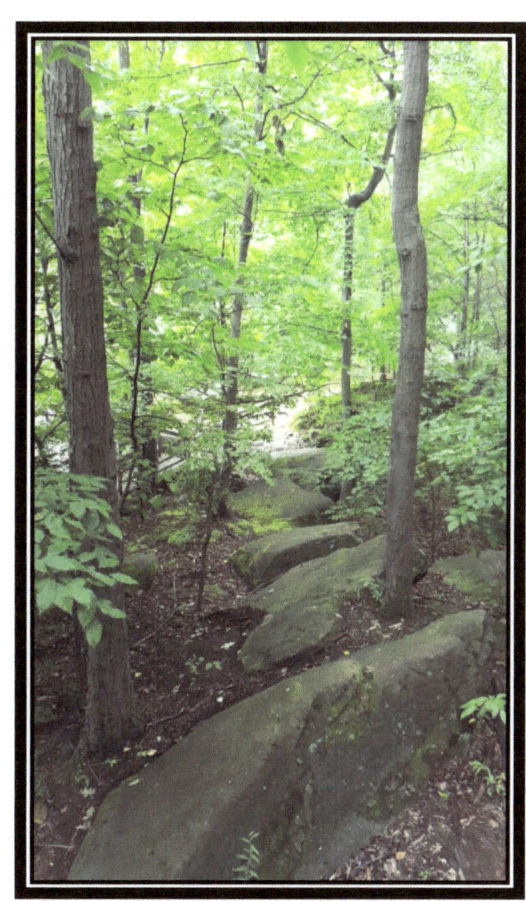

Photo: Janet Gauthier

J

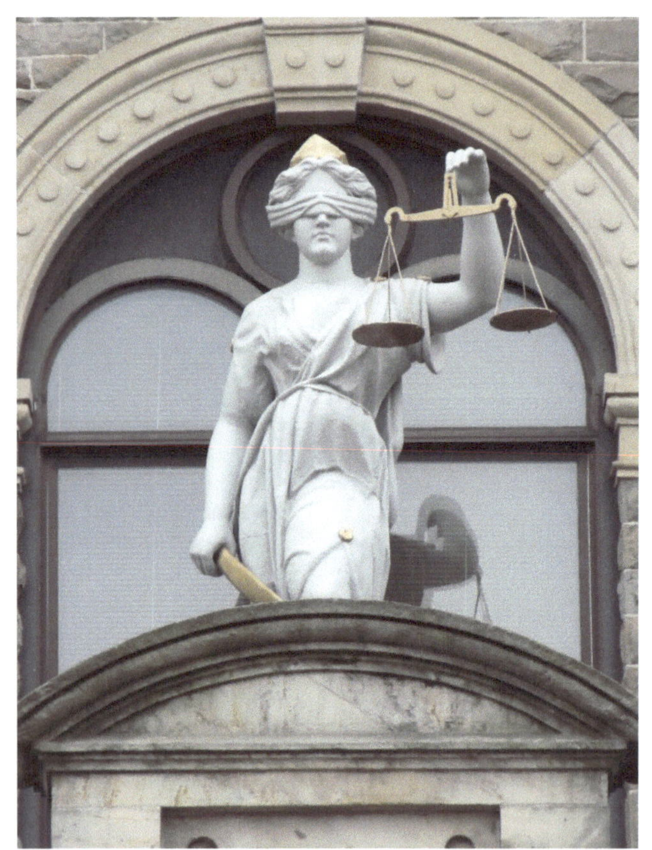

Photo: Janet Gauthier

The righteous care about *justice* for the poor, but the wicked have no such concern.

Proverbs 29:7 (NIV)

K

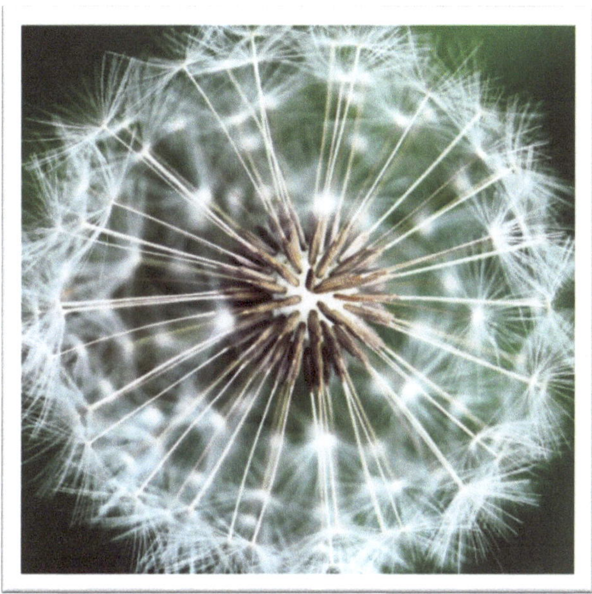

Photo: Annette Simon

When you're *kind* to others, you help yourself; when you're cruel to others, you hurt yourself.

Proverbs 11:17 (The Message)

L

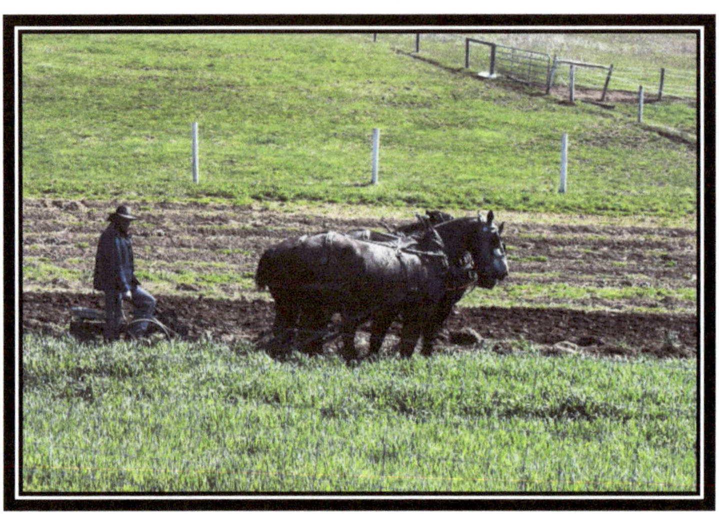

Photo: Annette Simon

A farmer too *lazy* to plant in the spring has nothing to harvest in the fall.

Proverbs 20:4 (The Message)

M

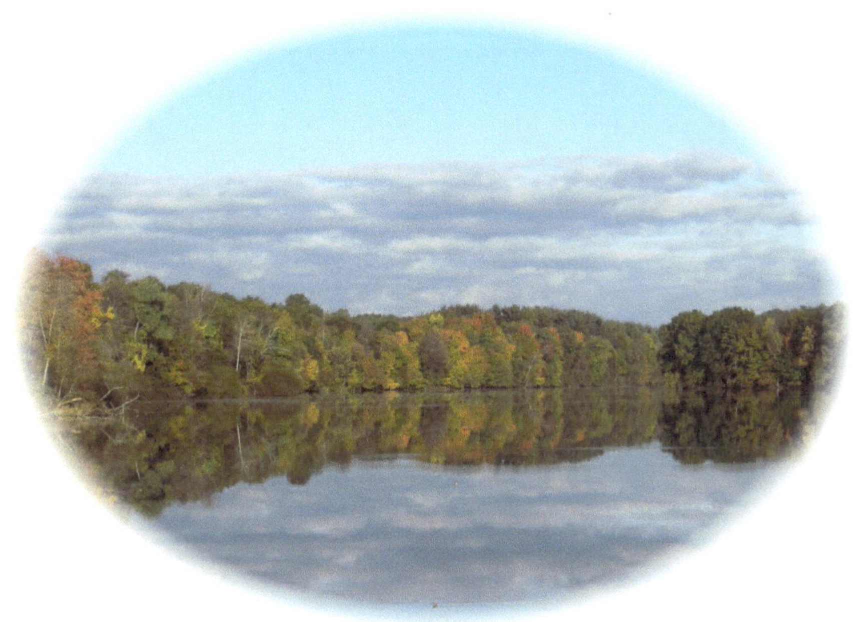

Photo: Janet Gauthier

Just as water *mirrors* your face, so your face *mirrors* your heart.

Proverbs 27:19 (The Message)

N

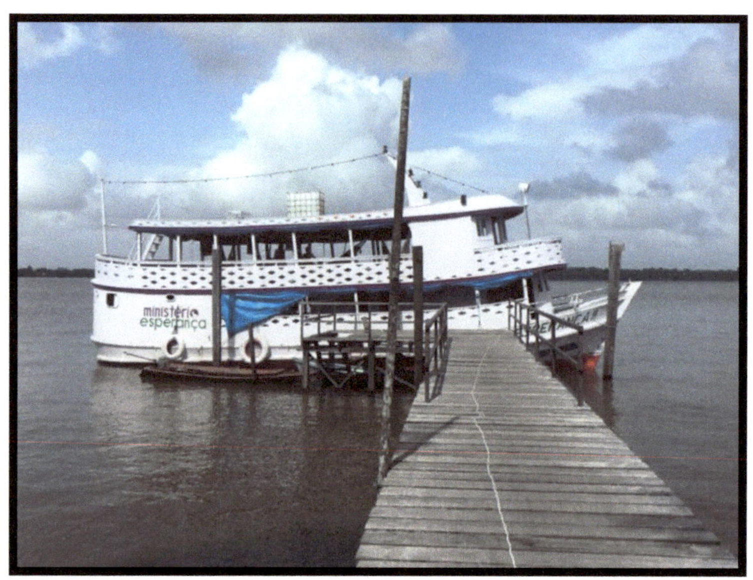

Hope Ministries Photo: Annette Simon

It is sin to despise one's *neighbor,* but blessed is the one who is kind to the *needy*.
Proverbs 14:21 (NIV)

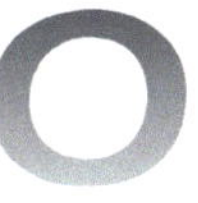

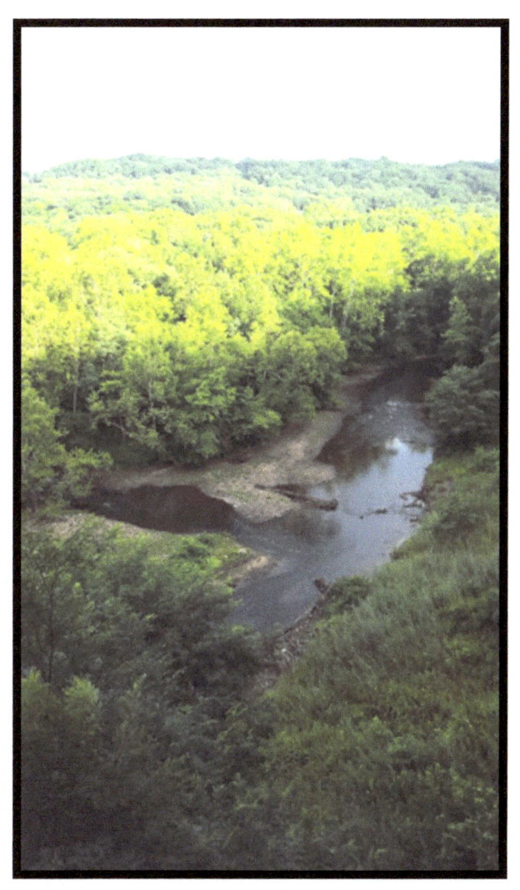

Photo: Janet Gauthier

A person's wisdom yields patience; it is to ***one's*** glory to ***overlook*** an ***offense***.

Proverbs 19:11 (NIV)

P

When a man's ways *please* the LORD, he makes even his enemies to live at *peace* with him.

Proverbs 16:7 (ESV)

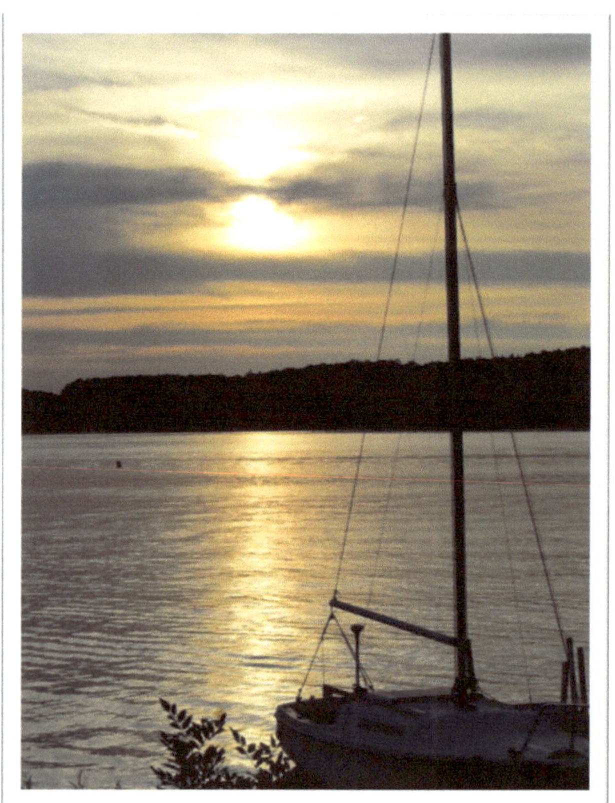

Photo: Janet Gauthier

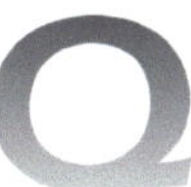

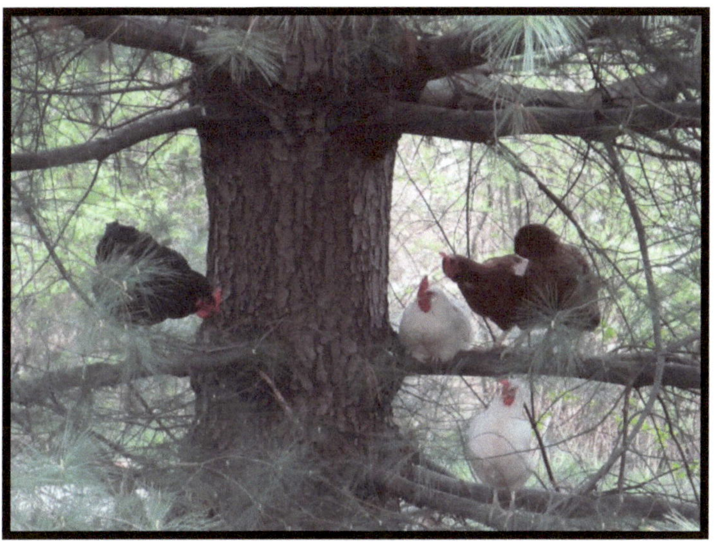

Photo: Janet Gauthier

A hot-tempered person stirs up conflict, but the one who is patient calms a *quarrel*.

Proverbs 15:18 (NIV)

R

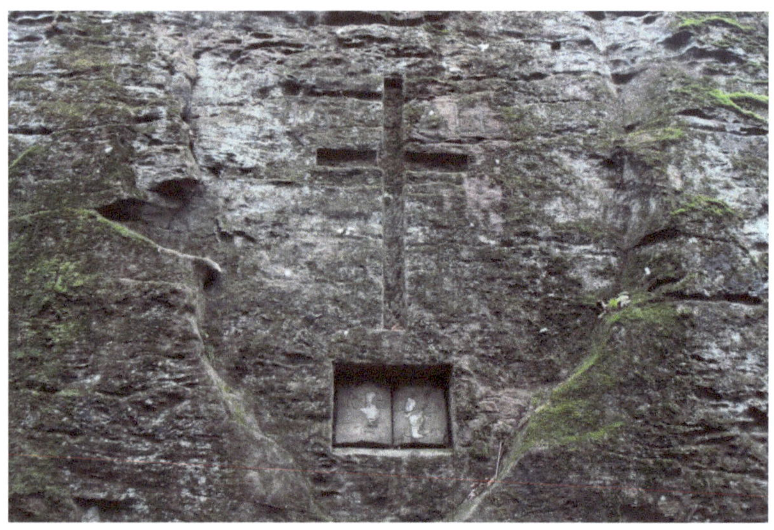

Photo: Annette Simon

Whoever pursues *righteousness* and kindness will find life, *righteousness*, and honor.

Proverbs 21:21 (ESV)

S

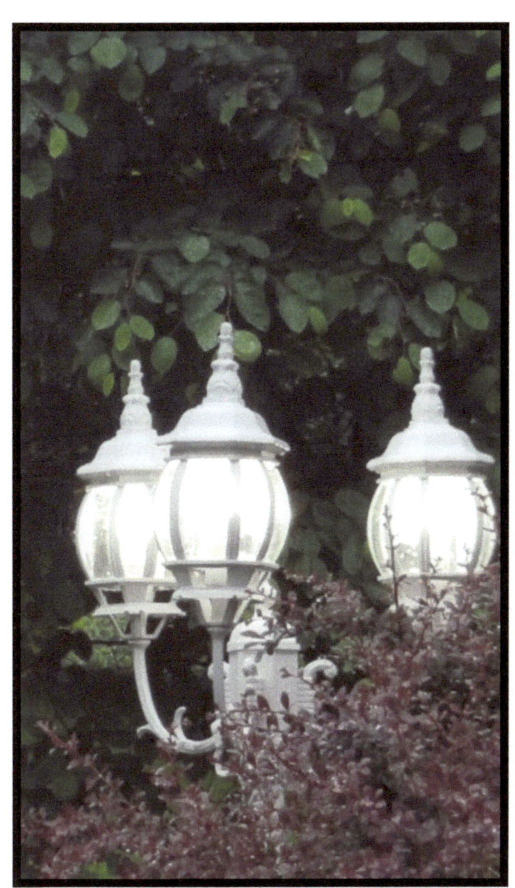

Photo: Janet Gauthier

The *spirit* of man is the lamp of the LORD, *searching* all his innermost parts.

Proverbs 20:27 (ESV)

T

Whoever keeps his mouth and his *tongue* keeps Himself out of *trouble*.

Proverbs 21:23 (ESV)

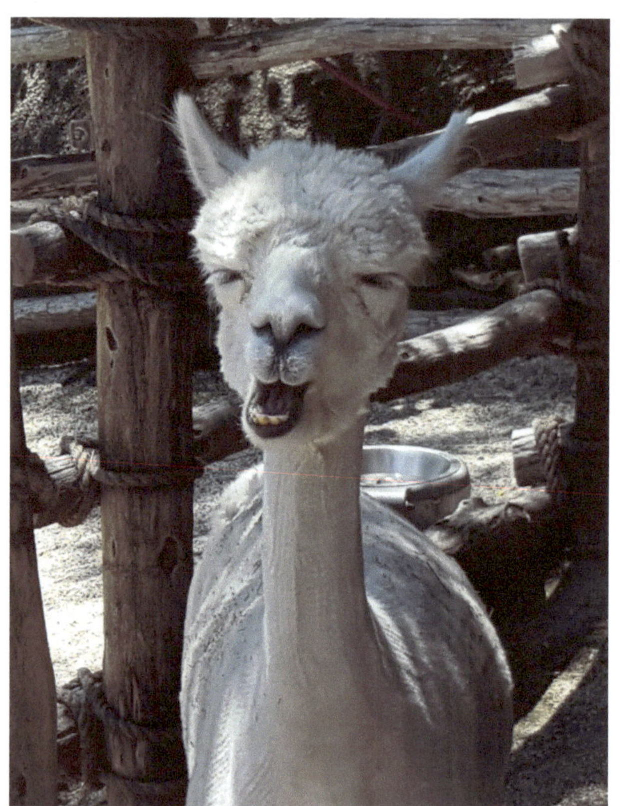

Photo: Janet Gauthier

U

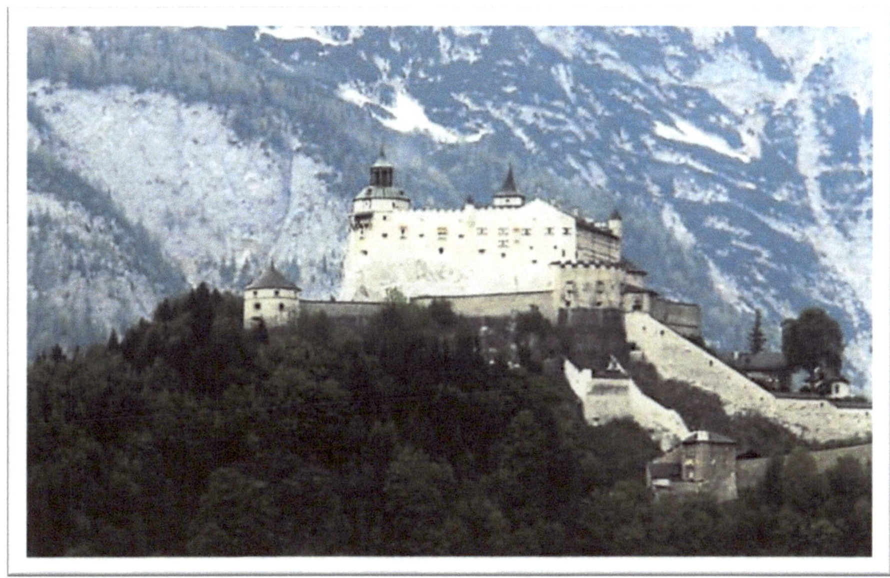

Photo: Annette Simon

A brother offended is more *unyielding* than a strong city

Proverbs 18:19a (ESV)

V

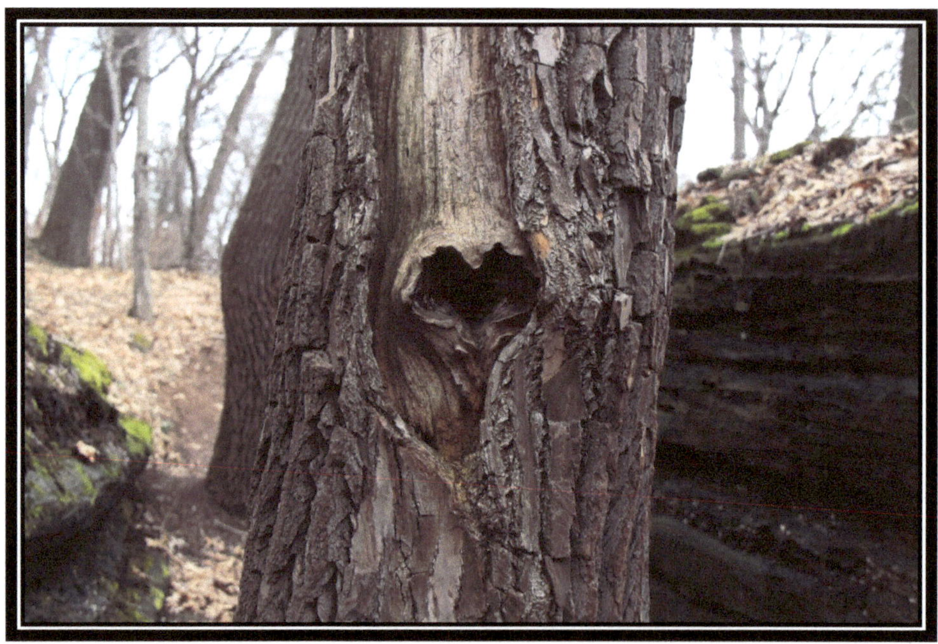

Photo: Annette Simon

Keep *vigilant* watch over your heart; that's where life starts.

Proverbs 4:23 (The Message)

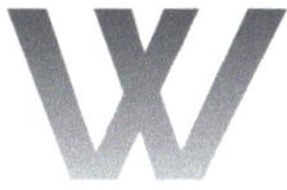

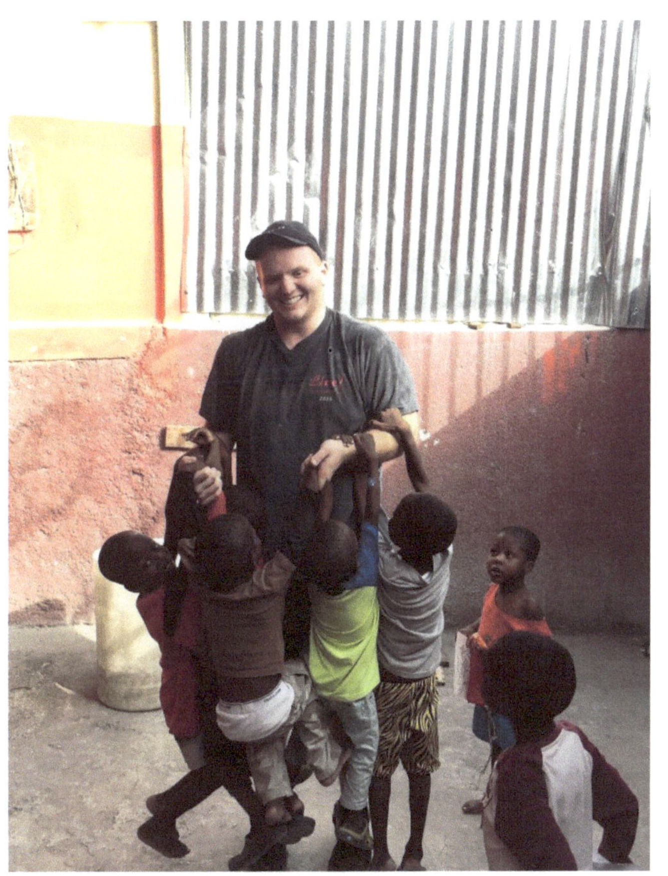

Photo: Janet Gauthier

Well-spoken words **bring satisfaction;**
well-done work **has its own reward.**

Proverbs 12:14
(The Message)

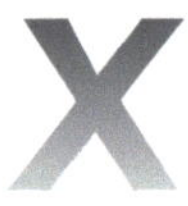

Anxiety weighs down the heart, but a kind word cheers it up.

Proverbs 12:25 (NIV)

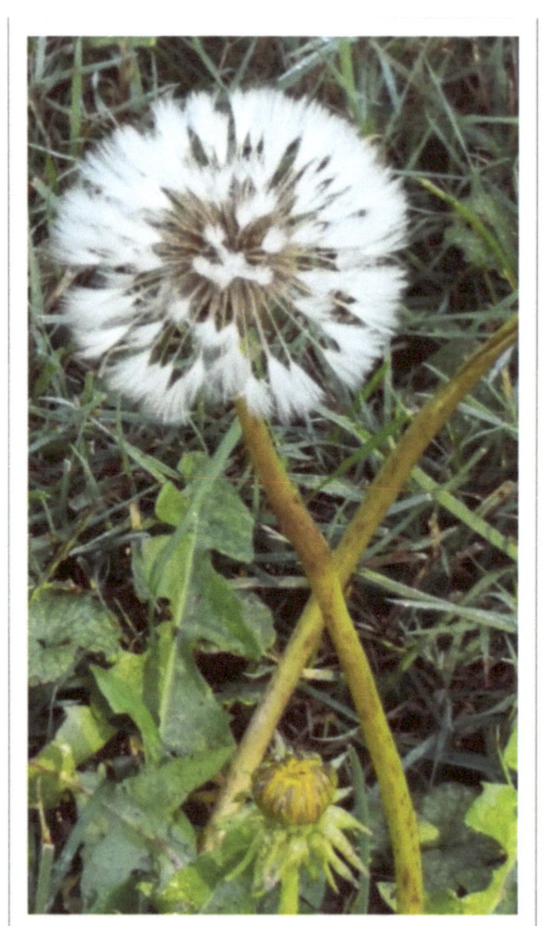

Photo: Janet Gauthier

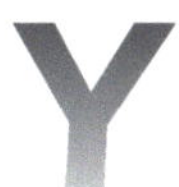

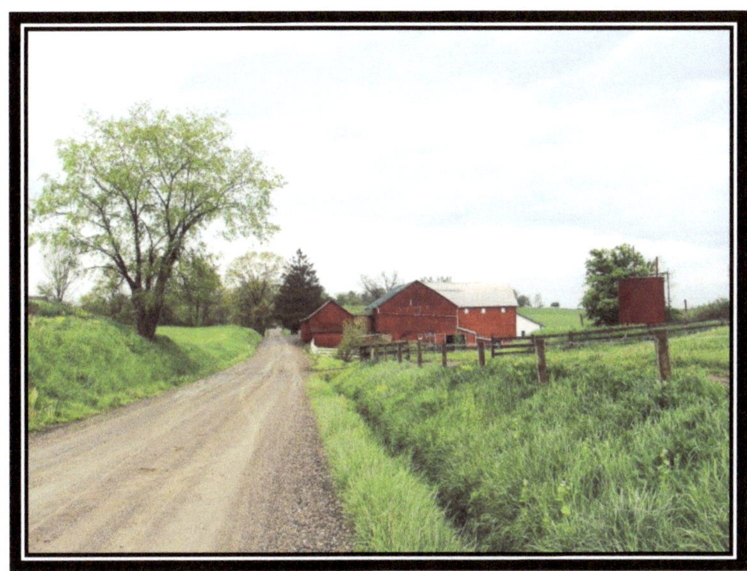

Photo: Annette Simon

In all *your* ways acknowledge Him [God] and He will make straight *your* paths.

Proverbs 3:6 (ESV)

Z

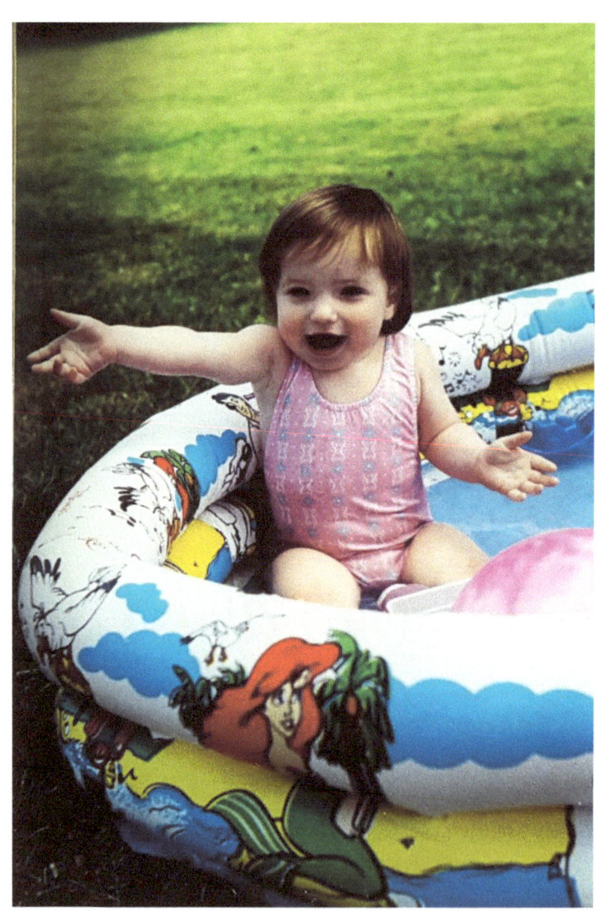

Photo: Janet Gauthier

Do not let your heart envy sinners, but always be *zealous* for the fear of the LORD.

Proverbs 23:17 (NIV)

www.ingramcontent.com/pod-product-compliance
Lightning Source LLC
LaVergne TN
LVHW070204110826
845147LV00002B/502

* 9 7 8 0 5 7 8 4 0 4 0 5 9 *